Elizabeth
Byers
Denver Pioneer

Elizabeth
Byers
Denver Pioneer

A NOW YOU KNOW BIO

J.v.L. Bell

Filter Press, LLC
Palmer Lake, Colorado

For my mom, Joyce Bell

ISBN: 978-0-86541-256-9
Library of Congress Control Number: 2019940231

Published by Filter Press, LLC
www.FilterPressBooks.com
Manufactured in the United States of America

Contents

Elizabeth Minerva Sumner Byers in 1872

1 "The Bane of My Existence"

Elizabeth Byers was four years old when her family traveled from Chillicothe, Ohio, to their new farm in Muscatine, Iowa. To reach Iowa, the family had to cross the Mississippi River. Unlike today, there were no bridges across the wide Mississippi. Instead, Elizabeth, or Libby, as friends and family called her, had to cross the river by ferry boat.

Ferry boats in the 1830s and 1840s were mud scows, which were large, flat-bottomed boats. They were propelled across the river by oars or poles and steered by a sweep, or rudder, that hung off the back of the boat. The sweeps extended far beyond the boat, making them heavy and difficult to use.

River crossings were dangerous and had to be made in places where the current wasn't strong. In bad weather, or rough current, the boat might be swept far downstream, or worse, **capsize**.

Scows were used to ferry people and products across rivers in the 1800s.

https://commons.wikimedia.org/wiki/File:Traveling-by-flatboat-engraving-by-Alfred-R-Waud.png

Libby's first memory was of climbing onto an old, rickety mud scow with the wind whipping the water into rough waves around it. As they crossed the Mississippi, the ferry rocked back and forth, and Libby was frightened "almost to death." As soon as the ferry reached the other side, Libby fell upon the white sand and kissed the beach, thankful to be alive. Libby would lead an adventurous life. This would not be her last dangerous river crossing.

Libby was born Elizabeth Minerva Sumner on August 31, 1834, in Chillicothe, Ohio. Her grandfather, Robert Lucas, was the governor of Ohio at the time. When her grandfather was appointed the first Governor of the **Territory** of Iowa, Libby and her family moved to Muscatine, Iowa, where she lived for the next sixteen years. Her father bought a farm and became a cattle merchant, buying and selling cattle in the Chicago stockyards.

Life in Iowa was not easy for Libby and her parents, Horatio Nelson Sumner and Minerva Lucas Sumner. Libby's home had no running water or electricity. As soon as children were old enough to help with chores, they did. Children often worked as hard as their parents. Their work was needed to help the family survive.

Libby was the third oldest of nine children. From a young age, she helped her mother care for her younger siblings and learned to cook, clean, and make many household items. Libby didn't have stores near her home. Instead, she and her family had to make most things the family needed. She and her sisters helped their mother sew their clothes, make soap and candles, and grow food in their garden. Her brothers helped their father tend the livestock, cut and split firewood, build furniture, and construct their home and a barn for their animals.

At that time, girls and boys often did different chores, but Libby remembers competing with her brothers. She bragged that there was nothing they could do that she couldn't, including shooting a gun.

When she was twenty years old, Libby married William Byers, a civil engineer and surveyor. The day they were married, she and her husband set out for Omaha, Nebraska, where William had started a surveying business. Their new home was on the **frontier** of the United States in an area that just months before had become the Territory of Nebraska.

Courtesy: Denver Public Library, Western History Collection, Z-2348

William N. Byers

During their trip from Iowa to Omaha, Libby experienced another frightening river crossing, this time across the Missouri River. When Libby was older, she wrote a short **memoir** about her life that she entitled *The Experiences of One Pioneer Woman*. This is what she wrote about that river crossing:

> I was married the 16th of November, and we came with our own team across country to Council Bluffs, Iowa. Rivers seem to have been the bane of my existence, and in attempting to cross to the frontier side of the Missouri River, we had a very bad time, not being able to take our team on the ferry, and landing after dark, after a windy and dangerous passage. The ferry boat started back and I was left alone on the bank of the river while my husband walked to Omaha, then a village of just a few buildings.*

---

*Quotations by Elizabeth Byers used in this book are from her unpublished memoir, *The Experiences of One Pioneer Woman*. The manuscript is part of the Western History Collection of the Denver Public Library.

William walked to Omaha to locate a new ox team, leaving Libby all alone on the bank of the river in the dark of night. She was very brave. Hostile American Indians roamed throughout the Nebraska Territory, and wild animals were all around. Fortunately, she was alone only a couple of hours before William returned. They traveled on to Omaha where they built a cabin and lived for several years. Libby and William had two children in Omaha. Their son, Frank, was born in 1855, and their daughter, Mary Eva or Mollie, was born in 1857.

Libby and her daughter, Mollie.

Denver Public Library, Western History Collection, Z-2351

A year after their daughter's birth, news of gold discoveries near Pikes Peak caused Libby and her husband to think about moving farther West. Libby knew her family would face many dangers. There were no towns in the Pikes Peak area and no family or friends. The wilderness area was home to **mountain men**, unfriendly Native Americans, and wild animals such as wolverines, bears, wolves, and mountain lions. In spite of the dangers, Libby and William wanted to head West.

Moving from Omaha, Nebraska, to a new settlement near Cherry Creek in sight of the Rocky Mountains wasn't a simple car drive as it is today. Instead, Libby's family had to travel the 540 miles across the Great Plains in a covered wagon. The Great Plains, also called the Great American Desert, is a flat, treeless region stretching from the Mississippi River to the Rocky Mountains. Sioux, Arapaho, Cheyenne, and other American Indian tribes had lived on the Great Plains for centuries. Huge herds of buffalo roamed the Plains, and **tornadoes**, dust clouds, and violent lightning storms were common.

Worst of all for Libby was the eight-week wagon train journey that would require crossing several dangerous rivers. There would be no ferries to take them across. They'd have to drive their wagons through the rivers.

Despite all their fears and worries, Libby and William decided to make the journey. Libby's life was about to get much more interesting and much more difficult.

2 Pikes Peak or Bust

On June 24, 1858, a group of men from Auraria, Georgia, led by William Greene Russell, discovered **placer gold** not far from where the Platte River meets Cherry Creek in present-day Englewood, Colorado. Can you imagine picking up gold nuggets in the rivers near Denver? Russell and his men mined about ten **troy ounces** of gold, worth about $200. Today, what they found would be worth over $6000. Excitement about their discovery sparked the **Pikes Peak Gold Rush**.

Getting to the Rocky Mountains from the East and Midwest, where most people lived, was difficult and dangerous. Why were so many people like Libby and William willing to risk the journey? One reason is that in 1857, the banks holding everyone's money began failing and people lost all their savings, causing an economic **depression**. Without money to buy and sell goods, workers lost their jobs as companies failed. Even farms had problems since no one had money to pay for wheat, corn, fruit, vegetables, and other products. Times were so difficult families had trouble feeding their children. Libby's family felt the effect of the depression when William's surveying business failed.

Know More!

When Libby married William Byers and moved to Nebraska Territory, there were thirty-one states in the United States. The rest of the country was territories. In a territory, there are few people and most of the land is owned by the federal government. The Territory of Nebraska included most of the land in present-day Nebraska, North and South Dakota, and Idaho.

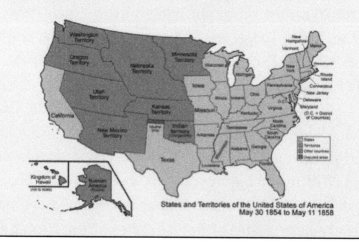

States and Territories of the United States of America
May 30 1854 to May 11 1858

Newspaper stories about the gold finds in the Rocky Mountains gave people hope. Many newspapers published exaggerated stories about Russell's discovery, but people were so desperate, they believed the exaggerations. Many who headed west thought they would get rich quickly by picking up gold nuggets lying on the ground. They planned to make their fortune and then return home to their families. It didn't matter to the gold seekers that the land belonged to Native Americans.

In the 1850s, Colorado was part of the Utah, Nebraska, New Mexico, and Kansas Territories. Much of the land had been given earlier by **peace treaty** to several American Indian tribes. Cheyenne, Arapaho, Sioux, Pawnee, Utes, and many other Native American tribes considered this country their home.

Most Americans knew very little about the Rocky Mountains. Despite their lack of knowledge, during the spring and summer of 1859, argonauts—gold seekers— stampeded west.

Like other people moving west, Libby and William decided they needed a way to make a living that did not depend on finding gold. They believed the best way to make money was not to search for gold, but to provide services to the miners in the growing towns.

The region would need a newspaper, and Libby thought William had the skill to start one.

Know More!

In 1851, the United States signed the Treaty of Fort Laramie with the Cheyenne, Sioux, Arapaho, Crow, Assiniboine, Mandan, Hisdatsa, Shoshone, and Arikara Indian Tribes. The United States gave the tribes land that included parts of present-day North and South Dakota, Montana, Wyoming, Colorado, Nebraska, and Kansas. The United States government also agreed to pay money, or **annuities**, to each tribe.

In return for land and annuities, the tribes pledged to be at peace with each other and with the United States. The Native Americans also agreed to allow roads to be built through their territories and promised safe passage for emigrants traveling along these roads. This treaty created a period of peace, which allowed settlers to cross Native American lands, but soon pioneers began to settle in those lands, creating conflicts and misunderstandings.

William agreed, although he also had another project in mind.

Today when people travel to a foreign country, they often buy a travel guide to tell them where to go and what to bring. Gold seekers in the 1860s left their homes to seek their fortunes in what seemed a foreign country in the West. They wanted a travel guide. Several men, who had never traveled to the Pikes Peak region, wrote guides, including William Byers.

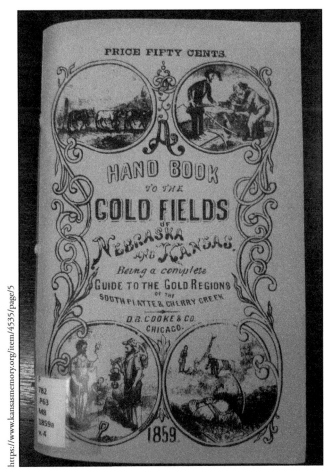

Cover of William Byers' Handbook

William wrote *A Hand Book to the Gold Fields of Kansas and Nebraska* and sold it to gold seekers for fifty cents a copy. He had traveled to California when he was younger, so he had crossed the Great Plains, but he was no expert on Colorado, nor had he ever visited any Colorado mines. Despite this, in his handbook he described the best trails gold seekers should take to cross the Great Plains and included lists of food and **provisions** they would need for the long journey. He even calculated costs. William estimated that if four men shared one ox team and a wagon, they could purchase all their mining supplies, six months of provisions, and a wagon and oxen for around $158 per person, or about $4,800 in 2019 dollars.

In the spring of 1859, more than 100,000 argonauts headed toward the Rocky Mountain gold fields. Many of these used William Byers' guide to help them. Some rode horses across the Plains, others traveled in wagons pulled by oxen, and some walked, carrying backpacks or pushing wheelbarrows filled with supplies. Few of these men understood the hardships that awaited them when they reached the new settlements near Cherry Creek or the mining camps in the Rocky Mountains.

Know More!

Prices in 1859 were much lower than today. In his handbook, William lists sugar at 9 cents per pound, bacon at 10 cents per pound, and flour at 35 cents for ten pounds. That means a miner could buy ten pounds of flour, three pounds of bacon, and four pounds of sugar for one dollar and one cent. In a grocery store, find these same foods and what they cost today. An increase in cost of goods is called *inflation* and is the reason $158 in 1859 is worth $4800 today.

3 The Rocky Mountain News

ROCKY MOUNTAIN NEWS.

THE MINES AND MINERS OF KANSAS AND NEBRASKA.

VOL. 1.   CHERRY CREEK, K. T., SATURDAY, APRIL 23. 1859.   NO. 1.

In 1859, newspapers were an important part of each community. At that time, there were no radios, televisions, or telephones. People wrote letters to friends and family, but it often took days or weeks for letters to travel from one state to another. Newspapers provided communities with local news, business advertisements, and stories from across the nation.

Using a large loan from Libby's father, William Byers started his newspaper business. While still in Omaha, he partnered with several men to form Byers & Company. Four of Libby's brothers joined in the newspaper venture. Byers & Company bought a printing press and added to their finances by convincing shopkeepers in Omaha to buy advertisements in the new newspaper.

Because the partners wanted theirs to be the first newspaper printed in the Rocky Mountains, they wrote almost half of the first edition—two full pages—before they left Omaha.

The newspaper needed a name. William Byers and his partners considered *The Cherry Creek Express* and the *Pikes Peak Herald,* but Libby suggested the *Rocky Mountain News,* and the name was settled. On March 8, 1859, William and his partners loaded their printing press and supplies into two covered wagons and headed west.

Libby and their two young children—Frank, age four, and Mollie, age two—stayed in Omaha with Libby's seventeen-year-old brother, Charles.

William reached the Cherry Creek settlements on April 17, 1859. He found a small community named Auraria on the southeast side of Cherry Creek. William Greene Russell had come from Auraria, Georgia, and in 1858, he named the new town after his hometown. Auraria is a Latin word meaning *gold.* Another settler, William Larimer, founded his own settlement on the northeast side of Cherry Creek and named it Denver City.

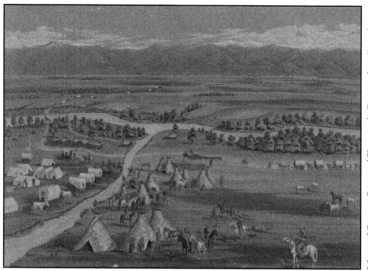

Auraria and Denver City in 1859

Auraria and Denver City in 1859 weren't like towns of today. Instead of paved streets, mud paths linked the few wooden buildings. Most residents lived in log cabins that had roofs of dirt and grass. Some miners hadn't bothered to build cabins and lived in tents or covered wagons. To make matters worse, the miners' turned their pigs, cows, horses, and oxen loose to roam freely through both towns.

A village of Arapaho Indians lived on the outskirts of Denver City. Native Americans spent winters camped near where Cherry Creek met the Platte River. They grazed their ponies on the rich prairie grasses near the rivers and hunted the buffalo, deer, and antelope that roamed nearby. This was their land, promised to them through treaties with the United States government. The gold seekers and the fast-growing towns now made their lives very difficult.

William Byers and his partners expected the *Rocky Mountain News* would be the first newspaper in the region, but they found they had competition. John Merrick had already set up his printing press and was busily working on the first edition of his newspaper, *The Pioneer.*

Byers & Company wanted to be the first and quickly went to work. They set up shop in the attic of "Uncle Dick" Wootton's store, saloon, and meeting hall. Dick Wootton's building was one and a half stories high, built of pine logs and whipsawed planks. The building had the only glass windows within 500 miles. Wootton was a tradesman and was happy to help Byers and his newspaper since they attracted customers to his saloon.

The whole town became interested in which newspaper would print first. Bets were made, and men hurried from one printing press to the other, spreading the news on each groups' progress. On Saturday, April 23, 1859, in a driving snowstorm, William hurried down from the attic clutching the first copy of the *Rocky Mountain News* hot off the press.

Byers' newspaper had won the race, but just barely. Twenty minutes after Byers handed out his first newspaper, Merrick produced the first issue of *The Pioneer*.

How much did a newspaper cost in 1859? William sold copies of his first newspaper for twenty-five cents each. Since this was mining country, he also sold copies for one pinch of gold dust.

Know More!

Paying in Gold

Miners in Colorado often paid for goods and services with "a pinch of gold dust." For instance, women charged one pinch of gold dust to wash a colored shirt, two pinches of gold dust to wash a white shirt.

But men, women, and children have different sized fingers. Did men pay more for goods than women?

Experiment to find out. Fill a tub with sandbox sand and pretend the sand is gold dust. Ask a man to pinch out twenty pinches of sand into one container. Ask a woman pinch out twenty pinches into an identical container. Weigh the two containers. Do they weigh the same?

How much more 'gold dust' did the man pinch out? Repeat the experiment with a child. How much less does it weigh if a child pinches out the gold dust?

After losing the race, John Merrick decided he would rather be a miner, so he sold his press and never published another issue of *The Pioneer*. He wasn't successful at mining and eventually became an editor for the *Rocky Mountain News*.

As William raced to publish his newspaper, there was trouble all around him. Thousands of men reached the Cherry Creek settlements. Many of these men spent a few days searching for gold, and when they didn't find

Source: Reprinted from *Beyond the Mississippi* by Albert D. Richardson, Bliss and Co., NY, 1867, p. 166.

' BUSTED, BY THUNDER !'

Busted, by Thunder!

gold nuggets lying on the ground like pebbles, they abandoned their search and returned home. Those more determined went deeper into the Rocky Mountains to look for gold, but initially, they too found nothing.

Broke and **disillusioned,** many men headed back across the Great Plains, telling everyone they met the gold rush was a **hoax.** William and a man named D. C. Oakes had written two of the most popular guidebooks. The men who couldn't find gold made up a new saying. *"Hang Byers and D.C. Oakes. For starting this damned Pikes Peak hoax."*

William responded to the men who thought he was responsible for their failure by writing this in his paper:

> All of this complaining has been brought about by the action of a few restless spirits who are no advantage to any country. They arrive in the vicinity of the mining region, stop for a few hours or a day or two, perhaps prospect a little in places the most unlikely in the world for finding gold, and, because they cannot shovel out nuggets like they have been accustomed to dig potatoes, they raise the cry that it is all a humbug.

By mid-May two-thirds of the people who had come to Denver had headed back to the States. Without people to buy his paper, the *Rocky Mountain News* would fail. William Byers was worried, but as the summer progressed, prospectors in the mountains west of Denver City found gold. George Jackson discovered gold in Clear Creek near present-day Idaho Springs, and John Gregory discovered gold near Black Hawk. Using sluices, or long troughs, John Gregory and his men mined $972 in gold, or more than $29,000 today, in one week.

The men brought news of their finds back to Denver, giving Byers & Company something to write about that rekindled the gold fever.

For the next six months, the *Rocky Mountain News* had no other newspaper competition in the Pikes Peak region, but the towns of Denver and Auraria were competing to attract the business of the gold seekers. Because Byers wanted his newspaper to be sold in both towns, he and his partners built the *Rocky Mountain News* office between the two towns, in the bed of Cherry Creek. This decision would prove disastrous a few years later.

With each new discovery of gold in the Rocky Mountains, the Cherry Creek settlements grew more prosperous. William believed the new towns would continue to grow, so he left the *Rocky Mountain News* in the care of his partners and returned to Omaha to move his family.

Libby packed up their belongings and in July of 1859, William hired a man to guide them west. Their first night on the trail, while Libby played her guitar to entertain her children, a group of American Indians arrived in their camp. Libby had seen Native Americans before, and like most women settlers, she was terrified of them. Newspapers exaggerated stories about Native American massacres against pioneers. Worst were the reports of women who had been **kidnapped** and forced to live with American Indians.

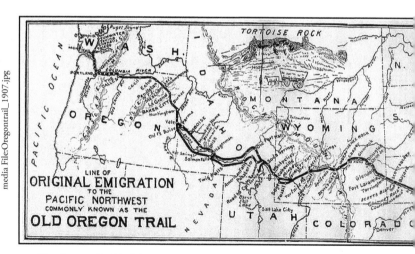

The Oregon Trail led thousands of settlers from Nebraska through Wyoming, Idaho, Oregon, and Washington between 1852 and 1906.

Although massacres did occur, *most* of the violence at that time was initiated by the white settlers and soldiers *against* the Native American population. American Indians, for the most part, were trying to defend their homeland as white settlers threatened their way of life.

Pioneers ignored the government treaties and settled on Native Americans' land. They killed so much of the wildlife—especially the buffalo—that Native Americans had nothing to eat. The settlers turned their cattle and horses loose to eat grass, leaving little for Native Americans' ponies. Finally, white settlers gave the Native Americans diseases such as smallpox

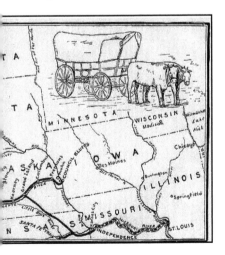

and cholera. Since the first Europeans arrived in North America, it is estimated that ninety percent of all Native Americans were killed by diseases brought by white settlers.

Although Libby was frightened by the Native Americans visiting her camp, she tried not to show her fear. Instead, she gave them something to eat. The Native Americans left, but their visit was an important reminder of the dangers she and her children were now facing.

For the next few weeks, Libby and her family traveled in a wagon following what we now call the Oregon Trail until they reached the northeast corner of present-day Colorado. There, they left the Oregon Trail and headed southwest following the South Platte River to Denver City. In his guidebook, William Byers had described the route by saying the streams were **fordable**, the road as "hard and smooth, without a stone or pebble to jolt the carriage," and the Platte River Valley as having "scarce a hill."

His description sugar-coated the difficult and dangerous journey.

The covered wagon held everything Libby owned, along with all their food and supplies, in a space smaller than a typical child's bedroom today. She and the children slept in the covered wagon, but everything else was done outside. Libby cooked on an open fire, washed clothes in the river, and kept her young children safe from rattlesnakes and wild animals.

Day after day, the sun beat down on them, rainstorms soaked them, and wind tore at their clothes and wagon. Despite these difficulties, for Libby the river crossings were the most dangerous part of the journey. Just before they reached Fort Kearney, Nebraska, a small military outpost on the Platte River, Libby experienced another frightening river crossing, which she wrote about in her memoir.

> When we came to the Platte River, of which there were at least three channels at Fort Kearney, I drove the team, the men plunging into the water from two to three feet deep. The quick sand was so bad in many places that a wheel would go down and the wagon careen, threatening to upset; perhaps a horse would be down and by the time the men could get them up the sand would be solid under their feet, and that is the way we worked across the first stream. The children were very badly frightened, clinging to me so I hardly knew I was driving, and you can imagine my consternation when I found there was another stream to cross that was equally as bad.

After traveling 185 miles in the covered wagon, Libby and William became unhappy with the man they'd hired to drive the wagon. In Fort Kearney they met the agent in charge of setting up the Overland

Stage Company between Fort Kearney and Denver City. He offered to take the family to Cherry Creek. They readily agreed even though the Overland Stage Company had horses and coach stations in place but no stagecoaches. Instead, the family would travel in a two-seated buckboard wagon.

The journey wouldn't be comfortable, but the buckboard could travel much faster than a covered wagon, cutting down the time it took for them to reach the Cherry Creek settlements. Normally, travel between Omaha and Denver took two months, but by traveling in the buckboard, the family hoped to reduce that time by almost half.

A buckboard is a simple four-wheeled, open-air wagon pulled by a team of two or four horses. Libby sat in the back seat and held her two young children. William and the driver rode in the front seat, guiding the horses across uneven and unpaved roads that sometimes were little more than a path.

During the 365-mile journey from Fort Kearney to the Cherry Creek settlements, the family traveled day and night, stopping only when they reached stagecoach stations, usually about every ten miles. Most stagecoach stations were simple, single-room **sod houses** with corrals for livestock. The stagecoach stops lasted between ten to forty minutes, often just enough time to change horse teams. On the longer stops, the family had time to buy a meal before the tired horses were replaced and the driver was ready to go.

Libby found meals at stagecoach stops tended to be the same, regardless of time of day: bacon, eggs, and biscuits served with coffee or tea. A few stations offered extra foods such as dried peaches or apples and wild meat.

On August 7, 1859, the Byers family reached Cherry Creek. Exhausted, Libby climbed from the wagon and later said she felt like she was "the advance guard of civilization." Libby's life had changed forever, and in this new frontier, many adventures and many more hardships awaited her.

Source: Beyond the Mississippi by Albert D. Richardson, Bliss and Co., NY, 1867, p. 186.

Seven Views of Denver, Colorado 1859, printed in a book entitled Beyond the Mississippi *in 1867, shows an Indian Village on Blake Street and William Byers'* Rocky Mountain News *office.*

4 Life in the Shadow of the Rocky Mountains

W hat were Denver City and Auraria like when Libby arrived? Albert Dean Richardson, who visited Denver and Auraria during the summer of 1859, described the towns as "a most forlorn and desolate-looking metropolis" with men dressed in "slouched hats, tattered woolen shirts, buckskin pantaloons and moccasins."

Both settlements were rough **boomtowns** where women were so scarce that Richardson said, "the appearance of a bonnet in the street was the signal for the entire population to rush to the cabin doors and gaze upon its wearer."

Libby had grown up on a frontier farm, but she'd never experienced anything like the Cherry Creek communities. Among the gold seekers were Hispanics, Cheyenne and Arapaho Indians, trappers, gamblers, ruffians, and a few honest men. During her first few years of living in the shadow of the Rocky Mountains, Libby saw lawlessness, drunkenness, and a couple of **vigilante lynchings** when the pioneers took the law into their own hands. Her new home was a rough place to live and an even more difficult place to raise two small children.

At first, Libby and her family stayed in one of the few hotels in town. It was a crude frame building kept by Captain Sopres and his partner, Mr. Slaughter. There was no furniture or beds, so the Byers family slept on mattresses on the floor in the front room. At one point, Mr. Slaughter's son joked with Libby and said they should hang a quarter of beef in front of the hotel and name the hotel The Slaughter House.

Finally, the wagon with their belongings arrived and the family moved into their own home, a one-room log house with a board roof and a dirt floor. Libby didn't mind the dirt floor, but she refused to live in a cabin with a grass and mud roof. Grass and mud roofs leaked when it rained, and she didn't want her belongings ruined by dirty, dripping rainwater.

Libby was fond of pretty things. Throughout her life she decorated her homes with fine art and furnishings, but pioneers crossing the Great Plains had to bring everything they needed in a covered wagon. There was no room for anything but necessities. Over the years, the Oregon Trail became littered with books, furniture, fancy clothes, and other 'unnecessary' supplies. The journey was long and hard and the lighter the wagon, the better the chance of pioneers surviving and arriving at their destinations.

Still, women like Libby refused to leave all their precious belongings behind. They often brought fancy curtains, lace tablecloths, a Bible, family pictures, ornate candleholders, and even a few pieces of fine china. Libby's cabin had a dirt floor with grass roots sticking out that would sometimes trip her, but she still took pride in decorating her home with what she called her **worldly possessions.**

During her first few months living near Cherry Creek, Libby wrote, "In this one room house, I had many laughable experiences some, however, were pretty hard to bear. There is much that is pathetic in a pioneer's life, and much that is awfully funny. We often laughed through tears."

With friends and family so far away, many pioneer women were lonesome and homesick. The 1860 census reported 34,277 settlers living in the Colorado

Territory, but less than five percent were women. Libby believed she was the eighth woman settler in the Cherry Creek settlements.

One day, William came home and announced he'd invited their friends—the Solomon Brothers, Colonel Tappan, and Colonel Dudley—to dinner. Libby's heart stood still. How could she ever cook for those gentlemen in this rough cabin? Initially she wasn't sure what to do, but she did have some fruit cake and peach preserves. She owned a milk cow, so she could make cream. Uncle Dick Wootton's store had supplies, but still, how could she cook for so many men?

All day Libby worked and when the men arrived, she began by showing off her few nice belongings. Then, she asked the men to help prepare the meal: one ground coffee, another set the table, a third cut bread and put out the pickles. The last guest helped her cook the steaks. This was very unusual because unlike today, men seldom helped with "women's work." During the many years they lived in Denver, Libby and her husband made many friends and enjoyed their social gatherings. In those early years, everyone lived much the same, all in difficult situations, but they all made the best of it.

"Making the best of it" was a pioneer attitude Libby kept for the rest of her life, especially during the difficult times.

By November they'd moved to a large log house with the printing office occupying the front room. Libby and her family lived in the two rooms in back. As she had done in her dirt-floored cabin, Libby decorated her new home and often entertained local **celebrities**. Guests at one dinner party were early **pathfinders**—Ceran St. Vrain, Jim Baker, Kit Carson, and James Beckwith (also known as Jim Beckwourth). Libby had all the food prepared and was ready for guests, but when the party arrived, she discovered something she hadn't expected.

> But when our guests arrived, and I found that one of them, Jim Beckwith, was a colored man, my aristocratic Virginia blood rather boiled, because I hadn't been used to sitting at a table with a colored man, and I hardly knew what to do, but almost instantly decided that there was but one thing to do and that was to ignore it altogether and treat them all alike, which I did.

BECKWOURTH.

Mountain man, scout, and trapper James P. Beckwourth.

This was a remarkable attitude for an American woman before the Civil War. At that time, many white Americans knew little about African Americans other than they were slaves. Even abolitionists, who worked to abolish slavery, would seldom sit down for a meal with an African American.

A good example of this was Dr. John Doy, a Kansas abolitionist. He'd fought and risked his life to help slaves escape to freedom. In January 1859, Dr. Doy was helping eleven African Americans escape from Lawrence, Kansas, when his party was captured by pro-slavery advocates. They were taken to Weston, Missouri, where slavery was legal. To punish Dr. Doy, his captors required him to sit at a breakfast table with the African Americans he'd been trying to save. Despite being an abolitionist, Dr. Doy refused to eat with the people he'd risked his life for.

As the population grew, Libby enjoyed many dinner parties with friends, but during that first winter, as prospectors flocked back from the Rocky Mountains, Libby noticed many miners suffering from lack of food, adequate housing, and illnesses. She saw a need and knew she must do something about it.

5 A Woman of Compassion and Action

As the winter of 1859-1860 grew colder, thousands of filthy, bedraggled men straggled into Auraria and Denver City. The men had spent the summer and fall **prospecting** for gold in the Rocky Mountains. Many returned without a cent to their names. They were living in tattered tents and ramshackle shacks, unable to afford food, fuel, or warm clothes.

Throughout her life, when Libby saw a problem, she figured out how to solve it. She spoke with her women friends and together they established the community's first **charitable** organization—the Aid Society, later called the Ladies' Union Aid Society. The sixteen women who started the Society decided to keep the society nondenominational, meaning it wasn't associated with a specific Christian church. The

Society's stated purpose was to "give aid and comfort to those in need."

Libby was chosen president of the Aid Society and during their first meeting—held in her home—the organization collected $60 in donations. The following day, a gentleman donated a $20 gold coin. Now, the women could get to work. They used the donations to open a soup kitchen and provide medical services. Each woman donated her time and skills, working at the soup kitchen and sewing underwear and warm night shirts for those in need.

Fourteen years later, in 1874, Libby and her friend Margaret Evans, the wife of the former territorial governor, John Evans, reorganized the society into the Ladies' Relief Society to help widows and elderly women. Women without husbands often had difficulty supporting themselves. Two years later, the group had raised enough money to build the Old Ladies' Home, for older poor women who would otherwise be homeless. By 1889, the society had grown large enough to help around 2,600 people each year.

On April 5, 1860, Denver City and Auraria joined to become one town, named Denver. It was still a rough frontier town filled with violence and **vice**. While Libby worked to help the poor and destitute, William wrote stories about the town's crime, condemning robberies, murders, and the rough and lawless men he called Bummers.

The Bummers often didn't like what he wrote. One of his stories got him kidnapped and almost killed.

In July of 1860, a fancy gambler named Charley Harrison shot and killed a well-liked blacksmith named Charles Stark. The fight began because Harrison—a **Southern sympathizer**—insulted Charles Stark, who was a former slave. The killing was considered a barfight, and Charley Harrison wasn't punished.

Outraged at this and other activities of Charley Harrison, William wrote a seething article on July 25, saying, "The man who has shot down an unarmed man, and then repeats his shots, while his victim writhes at his feet, until the charges of his pistol are exhausted— even if justified in the first act, is unfit to live in, and an unsafe member of a civilized community."

In addition to attacking Charley Harrison that day, Byers criticized the "rowdies, ruffians, and bullies" of Denver. His **scathing** attack on the Bummers, along with his demands for justice, caused many people, including Libby, to worry about his safety.

Judge Seymour Wagoner worried about an outbreak of violence and spoke with both Byers and

Harrison. The judge presented enough evidence in favor of Harrison that Byers backed down and **retracted** his earlier accusation. Harrison was satisfied, but unfortunately, the dishonest, drunken Bummers were still angry.

A mob of Bummers headed to the *Rocky Mountain News* office, which was now located in a building on stilts in the middle of Cherry Creek. William Byers was no stranger to trouble. He always asked prospective employees, "Can you handle a gun?" and felt an employee who was a good shot was more valuable than an experienced printer. Still, he wasn't prepared when Bummers broke into his office, dragged him to his feet, and held a cocked revolver to his head.

"What can I do for you, gentlemen?" William asked.

The Bummers insisted William come with them to Harrison's gambling hall, The Criterion. Their leader jammed his Colt revolver against William's head and said, "Byers, I got a good notion to air your brains right here and now."

The editor remained calm as the Bummers took him to Charley Harrison. Harrison hadn't known of the Bummers' plan, and he immediately realized William was in danger. He convinced the Bummers to let him talk with William alone. In the back room of his gambling hall, Harrison helped William escape.

Charley Harrison had saved his life but as William **hightailed** it back to the *Rocky Mountain News* office, the Bummers chased after him and soon bullets were flying. A window in the *News* office was shattered, and two Bummers were shot. After this incident, Libby noticed her husband never came home from the office without wearing a disguise. Several times she warned him about men hiding behind buildings, waiting to ambush him.

Despite this excitement, Libby continued to help the poor. When she needed money for her charity, she wasn't shy about asking—even in gambling halls like Charley Harrison's Criterion.

One day the Ladies Relief Society needed more money and appointed Libby and Mrs. John Pierce to find it. Libby went to the *Rocky Mountain News* office and told her husband she planned to raise $500 by four o'clock.

"You never will do it," he told her.

After borrowing a long pocketbook to hold the money, Libby left the News office and headed toward Denver's business district. Going up one side of a street and down the other, Libby stopped at each business. If it was a place she shouldn't enter, like a gambling hall, she would step just inside the door and flag down the **proprietor**. After explaining her business, she waited outside while the owner collected money from among the men in his establishment.

She found that gamblers were generous, and they treated her with courtesy and respect.

At a grocery store, the proprietor heard her request and said, "Well, I think it is time you were getting around [to] trying to do something. The people would all starve to death if you didn't." The man gave Libby $25, worth about $750 today.

At four o'clock, when Libby returned to her husband's office, she had $519 dollars in the pocketbook.

Libby and the Ladies' Relief Society branched out and continued to grow in their good works. They organized and opened the Industrial Home for Working Girls, helped organize a free kindergarten for Denver's children, and built and ran the Denver Orphans Home. Libby was also active in starting the Young Women's Christian Association and later, in 1893, she organized the Working Boys Home and School to keep poor boys out of trouble. The home was later renamed the E. M. Byers Home for Boys, in her honor.

The E. M. Byers Home for Boys provided shelter and education to homeless or orphaned boys.

Like most women of her time, Libby's church and religion were important to her. In 1860 she helped raise money to build St. Paul's Methodist Church, Denver's first Methodist church, and was president of the first church fair where they raised $1,500 in one evening. Today, a church would need to raise $24,000 in one evening to match the amount raised by Libby that evening.

Perhaps more interesting was her generosity in supporting any church—not just her own. When the Unitarian Church lacked decorations for the dedication of their new church building, Libby brought items from her own home for the church to use. Later in her life, she was a founding member of the Woman's Club, the Women's Press Club, and on the Board of Directors of Denver University.

Her generosity and kindness made her well liked in her community. Her caring attitude was remarkable, especially knowing the heartache, loneliness, and pain she experienced throughout her life.

6 Fire, Floods, and Death

Life for early pioneers was hard, and although Libby had more money than most, her life had many challenges. In June 1860, she and her family moved to a new house with windows, muslin-lined walls, and a finished floor. Her new frame house had two stories—a huge improvement from her earlier one-room cabin with a dirt floor. Libby's third child was born in the new house.

In October, a fire broke out in the upper story of the house. Libby was working downstairs and had the new baby with her—normally the child slept upstairs in the crib. Libby grabbed the infant and they miraculously escaped. The baby's crib, along with everything else in her home burned, including all of Libby's worldly possessions.

Libby was thankful she and her children had survived the fire. Death was common in this wild frontier and would soon be knocking on her door.

Charles Sumner, Libby's eighteen-year-old brother, arrived in Denver the following spring. The young man found a job as a Pony Express rider. The Pony Express was a network of riders that carried letters and newspapers across the frontier from San Francisco to New York. Riders transported mail bags, switching them from horse to horse every ten to twelve miles, and passing their bags on to a new rider after covering 75 miles without stop. Until the telegraph wires were in place, the Pony Express was the main means of communication between frontier towns and the rest of the States.

Within a month of his arrival, Charles fell ill with Mountain Fever. *Mountain Fever* was a term that described many illnesses, including altitude sickness and a fever transmitted by ticks. Libby asked a doctor to treat him. The doctor gave Charles medicine, but it seemed to make Charles sicker. After several days of not taking the medicine, Charles was still doing poorly. The doctor told Libby to give him a double dose of medication. After taking the large dose, Charles went into a **coma** and died. After his death, Libby learned the doctor had made a mistake. The doctor prescribed **morphine** instead of **quinine** and the medication had killed Charles.

Libby had not fully mourned her brother's tragic death when, two months later, her baby, who had so miraculously escaped the house fire, died. Libby wrote in her memoir, "This was a time to try men's souls, but our staunch friends stood in back of us, and but for the loyalty of friends, we should have been desolate indeed."

Friends and community members supported each other because everyone—even those well off like Libby and her family—experienced hardships. In the early hours of April 19, 1863, a fire broke out in the Cherokee House, a saloon at 15th and Blake Streets. Since most structures in Denver were built of dry, **resin-rich** pine wood, the fire quickly spread. In less than two hours, the business district east of Cherry Creek was a blackened waste. The fire burned more than seventy buildings—almost a third of Denver.

After the fire, Denver enacted a "brick ordinance" requiring all new construction to be made of fire-resistant materials such as brick. Today, most of the surviving older buildings in downtown Denver are made from a locally manufactured red-brown brick. Some of these long, narrow brick buildings are still standing along

lower Blake, Market, and Wazee Streets. William Byer's
Rocky Mountain News office wasn't damaged in the fire
of 1863, but a year later, during the 1864 Denver flood,
it wouldn't be so lucky.

To escape the grime of Denver, Libby and
William built a new home in the country, near the part
of Denver now known as Valverde. They spent several
happy years in this home. William grew a garden filled
with watermelon, and he built the largest ice box in the
area. At that time, there were no refrigerators, so people
used ice to keep food cold. Friends visiting the Byers
home were often served cold watermelon.

Know More!

To keep food from spoiling, Libby and other pioneers,
stored food in small underground rooms (root cellars)
and in iceboxes. Iceboxes were kept cold by placing large
blocks of ice in them. The blocks of ice were cut from local
lakes during the winter and stored in large, thick-walled
buildings called ice houses. The owners of ice houses
sold and delivered blocks of ice to homes during the hot
summer months.

The home bordered the Platte River, so the
family enjoyed fresh clean water and lots of shade
trees. Unfortunately, on May 19, 1864, a huge flood

caused the Platte River to rise and the floodwaters stranded Libby and her family in their house. They prayed for rescue as water poured in through their front door.

Unusually heavy rainfall in May 1864 caused the **headwaters** of Cherry Creek and the **tributary streams** that flowed into the Platte River to swell. For as long as Libby had lived in Denver, Cherry Creek had had very little water, and like most settlers, she considered it a dry creek. Many buildings, including the *Rocky Mountain News* office and the Methodist church, were built on stilts in the bed of the creek. Others were built very close to its banks.

Little Raven, an Arapahoe Chief, warned William that Cherry Creek would sometimes flood and that his building location was bad. William ignored the warning. Until the evening of May 19, the settlers had never seen Cherry Creek as anything but a small trickle of water.

The eastern plains of Colorado have a semi-arid climate, meaning the area receives more rainfall than a desert but not as much as areas with plentiful rain. When heavy rains fall in an arid region, the soil cannot absorb all the water. Instead of seeping into the ground, the water flows down hills and gullies, turning small streams into raging rivers. Larger rivers flood and quickly grow 10-to-50 times their normal size.

On the evening of the flood, residents of Denver thought little of the heavy rain even though Cherry Creek and the Platte River had more flowing water than usual. Denverites enjoyed a beautiful rainbow just before the sun dipped behind the Rocky Mountains. The Byers family were awakened in the early hours of the morning by a tremendous roar.

It sounded like a steam engine train, or maybe a tornado, was bearing down on the town.

Huge waves of water crashed down Cherry Creek and spilled over the banks, flooding Denver. The waves were ten to fifteen feet high and destroyed anything in their path. The water uprooted trees, demolished the low wooden bridges that spanned Cherry Creek, and swept away many of the buildings lining the small creek. The new Methodist church was torn from its **foundation**, homes disappeared, and William Byers' *Rocky Mountain News* office was swept away.

Several of William's employees were sleeping in the news office. They jumped out windows and swam for their lives. Fortunately, they were able to reach the shore safely before the building disappeared.

A view of West Denver C.T. during the flood in 1864

The 1864 Cherry Creek Flood destroyed homes and businesses, including the offices of the Rocky Mountain News.

Financial losses for Byers and his partners totaled more than $19,000, or about $300,000 today. Altogether, losses from homes and businesses were estimated between $500,000 and $1,000,000.

Unlike Cherry Creek, the dangerous fifteen-foot-high waves didn't flow down the Platte River, but the water level rose so high, new water channels formed. Before the flood, the Byers home had been located on the east bank of the Platte. As the river flooded, a new channel was cut, isolating the farm on a small island.

The water rose higher, flooding the house. Libby, William, and their children climbed onto tables. She told funny stories as William wrote a note saying his wife and babies were clinging to treetops. William sealed the note in a bottle and sent it downstream.

After almost a day of waiting, soldiers from Camp Weld arrived and built a skiff from an old wagon. They attached a rope to the crude boat so it wouldn't be swept downstream. Colonel Chivington, a Methodist minister who would later lead U.S. soldiers in the Sand Creek Massacre, oared the boat across the turbulent floodwater and reached the Byers farm.

Imagine Libby's terror. She'd given birth to a baby boy, James, in February, and her other two children were just nine and seven years old. It's unlikely any of them would survive if they fell from the skiff into the dangerous floodwater, but what choice did she have? Climbing into the tiny craft with her family, Libby experienced the worst river crossing of her life.

Colonel Chivington rowed them safely across the new channel. This kindness helped cement a friendship between Chivington and the Byers family. That friendship may have influenced how the *Rocky Mountain News* covered the Indian Wars of 1864-1865 that would soon disrupt life in Denver.

Know More!

Who Was John Chivington?

John Chivington, a Methodist minister, arrived in Denver in 1860. When the Civil War threatened Colorado, Chivington joined the military, becoming known as the Fighting Parson. Both the **Union** and the **Confederacy** wanted Colorado's gold to help finance the war. The Confederacy sent troops from Texas to take the gold from Fort Union. Colorado, a Union Territory, responded by sending troops to meet the Confederate soldiers. During the battle that followed at Glorieta Pass, John Chivington distinguished himself by destroying the Confederate supply train, forcing the Confederate army to retreat.

As the 1864 Indian Wars heated up, Colonel Chivington was the commanding officer at Camp Weld near Denver. In September, Chief Black Kettle, Chief White Antelope, and several other Arapahoe, Cheyenne, and Kiowa Indians friendly to the pioneers came to Denver seeking peace. They met with Governor Evans and Chivington and were sent to Fort Lyon, to camp on their reservation at Sand Creek. In November, Chivington led the 3rd Colorado Volunteer Cavalry Regiment and other military units to Sand Creek and massacred many of the Native Americans camping there, including Chief White Antelope.

Just before they attacked, it is reported Chivington said, "I believe it is right and honorable to use any means under God's heaven to kill Indians who kill and torture women and children. Damn any man who is in sympathy with them." Chivington ordered that no prisoners be taken. It is estimated that more than 300 Native American men, women, and children were slaughtered during the massacre.

It was a terrible massacre, yet at the time, when Chivington and his men returned to Denver, they were greeted as heroes. William Byers wrote favorable articles about them in the *Rocky Mountain News*.

7   Indian Wars

Since 1859 when hundreds of thousands of white settlers began arriving in the area that is now Colorado, the life of the Native Americans became increasingly difficult. Unlike the early mountain men, gold seekers didn't interact with the Native Americans and few learned to appreciate their way of life. The newcomers seldom learned the Native American languages and most thought of the natives as pests, or worse.

Miners also worried about the Native Americans' rights to the land they now considered their own. As early as October 11, 1860, *The Mountaineer*, a Golden, Colorado, newspaper, raised the issue of the Native American's rights to "the lands we are occupying." The newspaper article complained the Indians should "settle upon a reservation, and till the soil like white men."

Che Mountaineer.

Thursday, Oct'r 11, 1860.

Indian Matters.

We gave in our issue of last week a letter from the Junior Editor, Mr. Knox, written from the treaty ground at Bent's Fort. It seems that nothing was done effectually to extinguish the Indian title to the lands we are occupying so that a survey can be made, and settlers feel safe on the claims they are holding. Nothing but a verbal agreement was entered into for the Indians to give up the Platte, or any portion of it, and to settle upon a reservation, and till the soil like white men. Of

The atmosphere grew tenser when Denverites did little after Bummers brutalized Native American women living near Denver. With wild game more difficult to find, Native American men spent a significant amount of time away from their villages, leaving their women alone and vulnerable to attacks.

By 1864, skirmishes between Native Americans and settlers had become deadlier. The *Daily Mountain Journal*, Black Hawk's newspaper, printed a short article on March 19, 1864, that called for all-out war against the Native Americans. The article stated, "the Indians want to be killed off—that's certain" and "our new Maj. Generals and Brigadiers want to distinguish themselves."

It's difficult for us today to understand the attitudes of the settlers. **Prejudices** were strong, and Native Americans, along with African Americans, were considered and treated as lower class people. Because the Native Americans could not be controlled like African American slaves, they were also feared.

Settlers in the Colorado Territory were isolated from the rest of the United States. To travel back to their families in the East, settlers had to cross over the Great Plains. By mid-summer of 1864, most overland trails were no longer safe to travel because of Indian attacks. Freight wagons bringing much needed food and supplies were unable to cross the plains, causing prices in Denver to rise.

As this turmoil continued, the 1864 Denver flood destroyed thousands of dollars of supplies, increasing the settlers needs and fears. Territorial

Governor John Evans sent anxious letters to U.S. government officials begging for assistance and stating the settlers of Colorado are "at war with a powerful combination of Indian tribes, who are pledged to sustain each other and drive the white people from this country."

Governor Evans may have exaggerated the danger. Unfortunately, during this time period the United States was fighting the Civil War. It didn't have the men and resources to help with the conflict between the settlers and Native Americans. It was a dangerous situation that kept getting worse.

Following the flood, the Byers family was homeless. They had lived with their friends, Governor John Evans and his wife, Margaret, for ten days after their exciting boat ride through the floodwaters. Like many Denverites who'd lost their homes, the Byers needed a place to live. They had an advantage of knowing important people.

Before the flood, Governor Evans and Colonel Chivington had founded the Colorado **Seminary**, a Methodist college that years later would become Denver University. In 1864, the school was not yet open and the new building on 14th and Arapahoe became the Byers' home while they built a new house in Denver. They were living at the seminary when Denver experienced what was later called "The Great Indian Scare."

On June 12, 1864, the Hungate family, who lived about twenty-five miles east of Denver, were murdered by Native Americans. The deaths were horrific. The attackers tortured and killed Mrs. Hungate and her two small children. Tension between Native Americans and Denverites had steadily risen throughout the spring and when the scalped bodies were brought to Denver and put on display, the level of alarm rose to near hysteria. Farmers living around Denver fled to the protection of the city and the isolated pioneers waited for an attack.

Their fears appeared realized on June 16 when rancher William Shortridge rode frantically into town and announced that a large party of hostile Native Americans were headed toward Denver. Denverites believed the Native Americans planned to burn the city and kill everyone living in Denver. Church bells rang in alarm and Governor Evans initiated a 6:30 p.m. curfew. All able-bodied men were ordered to assemble and help build blockhouses and log fortifications just outside of town. The town prepared for an attack.

Years later, Libby described this day.

> While in the Seminary building we had the great Indian scare. Col. Fillmore was in charge of the troops at that time. He seemed the most frightened man in the village. He rushed the women and children to the old Mint building, where they were huddled in like sheep; a good many came to the Seminary building where I was. Col. Filmore rushed to me in a frenzy and said: "My God, woman, take your children and get down to the Mint." I said: "Colonel I am as safe here as at the Mint. If the Indians want my scalp they can take it right here."

Native Americans never attacked Denver—there had been no real threat—but this was just one more event that eventually led to the Sand Creek Massacre. At Sand Creek, Chivington with an army of 700 men massacred more than 300 Cheyenne and Arapaho, including women and children. The Native Americans were camped at Sand Creek because Chivington and Governor Evans had told them they would be safe there.

After the Sand Creek Massacre, many Native Americans tribes in the West did go to war. They'd seen the United States government make and break every treaty. Promises had been made and broken so many times the Native Americans no longer trusted the white man. The lies and the massacre at Sand Creek were the final insult. Enraged Native American tribes launched a real war against the settlers. For several years, travel across the Great Plains was very dangerous.

Despite the dangers, in the fall of 1866 Libby decided to take her children back to Iowa to visit her parents. Libby chose to travel by stagecoach across what was then known as the Butterfield Cut-off between Denver and Kansas City. She and her children were two days out of Denver, having supper at a stagecoach station, when Libby was given a letter. Mr. Butterfield, the manager of the route, informed her an earlier stagecoach had been captured and burned by Native Americans. He recommended waiting at that station until troops from Fort Riley arrived.

Libby and her three children—Frank, 11, Mollie, 9, and James, a toddler—were stuck. There were no phones at that time, so Libby was unable to contact her husband in Denver or let her family in Iowa know what had happened. There was also little extra room at the station for guests. Libby and her children slept in a covered wagon outside the small ranch building.

Also stuck at the station with Libby and her children were several other stagecoach passengers and a large wagon train made up of about forty **teamsters**. The teamsters had brought goods to Denver and were returning to the States. In Libby's memoir, she writes the men were armed, but they had no ammunition. They had probably sold all their ammunition—at a good profit—to frightened Denverites.

After three days of waiting, some of the male passengers spoke with Libby about going on. They reasoned they were no safer at this tiny ranch than on the road, but they left the decision to Libby. After all, she had three children under the age of eleven to consider. Libby approached the wagon boss of the teamsters and said, "You are going in the same direction that I am. I have decided to go on with the coach, and I want your outfit to accompany me."

The wagon boss was uncertain. Mr. Butterfield had ordered him to stay at the station. After a bit, Libby convinced him to leave. The following day the stagecoach, accompanied by the teamsters and their wagons, headed out.

Freight wagons move slower than a stagecoach, but the group stayed together. They were tense and worried, expecting to be attacked by angry Native Americans at any time. The first night out, they camped with the freight wagons circled around them. The wagons formed a **barricade** around the passengers, livestock, and stagecoach.

The next morning, their journey was interrupted when they spotted a white man running across the plains. Despite Libby's worries it was a trap, several of the men in her party went after him. Fortunately, it wasn't a trap and several hours later the men returned with the stranger.

The newcomer was **demented**, suffering from fright and lack of food and water. After giving the man food and drink, they learned the stranger was from the stagecoach which had been attacked and burned. He had managed to escape, only to become lost. Although frightened by the man's story, they continued down the road toward the spot where the stagecoach had been attacked.

That afternoon they camped, but as the night grew dark, they saw the light of a camp fire. Was it the camp of the soldiers coming to help them, or the Native Americans coming to attack them? They didn't know. Libby and her children waited fearfully as two brave men volunteered to find out. Later she wrote about this encounter:

> So two of the men started up for the camp, calling as they went, trying to make themselves understood when they got near enough, but didn't seem to be able to do so, and the noise of voices threw the camp into a panic. We could hear them call to put out fires and the orders from the men in command, and for a time it seemed thrilling in the extreme. Finally our men managed to make themselves understood that we were white people and friends, that we had the coach, so then they let us come into camp, restored the fire and lights, and we found it was the soldiers that were guarding the up coach which was coming to our relief.

They were rescued, but Libby never forgot the fearful journey. With the soldiers as guards, Libby and her children made it to Atchison, Kansas, without trouble. From there they took a boat up the Mississippi River to Muscatine, Iowa. She and her children spent the winter with her parents in the home she'd grown up in.

While they were in Iowa, eighteen-month-old James caught **pneumonia** and died.

The following spring, Libby headed back to Denver. She was accompanied by her brother, Jack Sumner, and her younger sister, Flora. The railroad now went as far as Fort Kearney, Nebraska, so Libby and her children traveled by train to the fort. From there, they joined a well-armed wagon train and, just as Libby had done eight years earlier, they followed the Oregon Trail along the Platte River. They stayed with the wagon train until they reached the North Platte and the cut-off trail to Denver.

The wagon train wasn't headed to Denver, so Libby, her brother and sister, and the children were on their own for the final leg of the journey. Each night they camped near stagecoach stations, hoping that would offer them some safety. Attacks by Native Americans were not the only danger on the trail. One evening, they were camped near a stagecoach station when a powerful thunderstorm struck. It had some of the most vivid lightning Libby had ever seen. The storm was raging around them when Libby heard an unusual noise. She alerted her brother, Jack, and anxiously they waited and watched. Lightning lit up the sky and they saw two men sneaking up to steal their horses.

Know More!

In 1866, when Libby's son, James, became ill with pneumonia, there was little doctors could do. Antibiotics, such as penicillin, wouldn't be discovered until the 1920s. Diseases such as cholera, smallpox, typhoid fever, dysentery, pneumonia, and yellow fever killed many people, especially young children. The 1860 census reported 63,873 deaths from these six diseases. Of these deaths, pneumonia caused 27,094. As can be seen from the notice below, people at that time didn't know what caused many diseases.

NOTICE.

PREVENTIVES OF

CHOLERA!

Published by order of the Sanatory Committee, under the sanction of the Medical Counsel.

BE TEMPERATE IN EATING & DRINKING!

Avoid Raw Vegetables and Unripe Fruit !.

Abstain from **COLD WATER**, when heated, and above all from *Ardent Spirits*, and if habit have rendered them indispensable, take much less than usual.

Libby's heart stood still. Without the horses, their trip to Denver would be much longer and much more dangerous. Jack fired his revolver and the men scrambled out of sight. The storm continued, but the men didn't return. After that experience, Libby made sure the horses were tied close to their tents at night.

After five days alone on the trail, they reached Denver. Libby was glad to be home. The town she entered was far different from the one she first saw in 1859. Denver had a steady and growing population, prosperous businesses, and stable buildings of red brick. It was a town that was here to stay.

8 Colorado Becomes a State

B etween 1859 and 1870, Denver was a "boom and bust" town. It swelled with gold seekers each summer and lost much of its population during the winter. The population that settled there stayed at around 4,000 to 5,000 until 1870, when the Denver Pacific Railroad stretched across the Great Plains and reached Denver. By then, the buffalo were gone, and the Native Americans had been forced onto reservations.

Denver continued to grow from a frontier town to a prosperous city.

When they first arrived in the Cherry Creek settlements, William Byers and many of the settlers wanted to govern themselves. In 1859, what is now the state of Colorado was actually part of Utah, Kansas, New Mexico, and Nebraska territories. In order to become a territory, William and other men living in Colorado had to petition the United States government for territorial status. This was granted to them on February 28, 1861.

A Territory has a governor appointed by the United States government, but it doesn't have representation in Congress. The first capital of the Territory of Colorado was in Colorado City, now part of present-day Colorado Springs. It was soon moved to Golden, and then in 1867, after much **lobbying** by William and other Denver men, the capital was moved to Denver.

In the Colorado Territory, women were allowed to own property, thanks to the passing of a Married Woman's Property Act. In other places in the United States, women could not own land, houses, or other property. Still, there were no women in the Territorial government and women couldn't vote in elections. People who thought women should be allowed to vote were called suffragists. Since the early 1800s, women suffragists had been fighting for a woman's right to vote. Libby was active in several suffragist organizations.

Ex-governor John Evans and others tried to introduce a woman suffrage bill in the Colorado Territory in 1868. His bill failed and it took several more tries, but finally in 1893, seventeen years after Colorado became a state, women won the right to vote in Colorado.

Know More!

In the early 1800s, most men in the United States had the right to vote, but not women. By the 1830s and 1840s, the woman's suffrage movement—women and men working to give women the right to vote—had gained enough strength that some men, especially those in western territories, were taking it seriously.

The Washington Territory introduced woman's suffrage legislation in 1848, but the bill was narrowly defeated. Finally, in 1889, the Wyoming Territory approved a constitution that included a provision granting women the right to vote. It wasn't until 1920 that the United States ratified the 19th Amendment to the Constitution and allowed women to vote.

After being a Territory for several years, people wanted Colorado to become a state. To become a state, the territory must again petition the federal government.

Unfortunately, in 1861, the Civil War between the Northern and Southern United States began. Because of the tensions between slave and non-slave states, Colorado was refused statehood. Even after the Civil War ended, it took many more years of petitioning, but on August 1, 1876, Colorado finally became a state. Colorado was the 38th state to become part of the United States.

In 1883, William and Libby built a beautiful new brick home on 14th Street. They lived in the house for six years before selling it to their friend's son, William Evans. He and his family lived in the house for many years. Today, the house serves as the Center for Colorado Women's History at Byers-Evans House. The address is now 1310 Bannock Street, because Denver street names have changed. Visit the museum to see how people lived many years ago.

The Byers-Evans House was built by William Byers for his family. It became the home of the William Evans family in 1889.

Now that Colorado was a state, it needed a capitol building. In 1889, the Colorado legislature authorized two million dollars for the construction of a state capitol.

The building would be made from Colorado products, including rose onyx **quarried** from Beulah, white yule marble quarried from Marble, Aberdeen granite quarried from Beaver Creek, and red sandstone from Lyons.

As she grew older, Libby was involved in the beautification of Denver. She knew many of the statesmen making the decisions on the design and construction of the state capitol. The capitol dome was originally covered in copper, which slowly **tarnished** as it was exposed to weather. Lawmakers considered replacing the copper with several other materials, but Libby fought and won to have the dome resurfaced in gold leaf, using Colorado gold. She lost the battle to have the front steps made of gray granite, and instead the steps were made of red flagstone.

Lawmakers decided to include stained-glass portraits of famous Coloradans in the capitol's dome. They planned sixteen stained-glass windows equally spaced around the dome and each window would represent an individual who had made significant contributions to Colorado's history.

Which sixteen people should be chosen?

Names were considered and slowly individuals were chosen. There was Colorado frontiersman Kit Carson and the beloved Reverend John Dyer who snowshoed from town to town, delivering sermons and the mail. Chief Ouray was included to honor his fight for peace between the Utes and pioneers. William Byers was honored for his promotion of Colorado through the *Rocky Mountain News*. Others were chosen, but lawmakers ran into a problem. They hadn't selected any women.

Colorado State Capitol photographed in 2018 by the author.

The Ladies Relief Society nominated Libby as the "wife of the editor of the first newspaper in Denver." The selection committee agreed and offered Libby the honor of a stained-glass portrait to be placed beside her husband's. She turned them down. She was proud of her husband and his accomplishments, but she was also proud of her own accomplishments. She didn't want the honor if it was offered because she was William Byers' wife.

She responded to the offer by saying, "While I gladly accord my husband every honor he is entitled to, and rejoice that he is so honored and appreciated by his fellow-citizens, I remember that he and I stood shoulder to shoulder through all the trials and hardships of pioneer life, and feel that I ought not stand wholly in the light of reflected glory."

Photo by author, 2018.

A stained-glass portrait of William N. Byers hangs in the Colorado State Capitol.

In Libby's place, Frances Wisebart Jacobs, who is known as Denver's "Mother of Charities" for her work on behalf of the poor and ill, was honored.

William Byers died in 1903. He had been editor of the *Rocky Mountain News* for nineteen years. After his death, Libby remained busy, active in charities and her church. She died in 1920 and was buried beside William in Denver's Fairmount Cemetery.

Photo by author, 2018.

The Byers' family burial plots in Fairmount Cemetery in Denver, Colorado.

Libby lived in Denver six decades. Although she never searched for gold, she was a true argonaut in spirit and as important as her husband in turning Denver from a boom-and-bust community to the capital of a new state. While her husband promoted Denver, sometimes for his own interests, Libby spent her life making Denver and Colorado a better place to live.

J. Simms wrote a multi-page, hand-written document entitled "Delineation of Character of Mrs. Wm M Byers" dated October 10, 1876. A delineation is a description of a person by someone who knows them. In his delineation, Simms described Libby by saying, "Your aim is to be good and to do good and live for others more than yourself." Even in 1876, Libby was recognized for her generous spirit. Libby's acts of charity and her assistance to the poor have lasted long after her death. She is remembered as one of Denver's most respected and admired pioneers.

Denver Public Library, Western History Collection, Z-2311

Libby Byers surrounded by floral gifts on her 80th birthday.

Timeline

08.31.1834 — Elizabeth Minerva Sumner was born in Chillicothe, Ross County, Ohio.

1838 — Family moved from Ohio to Iowa.

1854 — Libby married William N. Byers, and they left for Omaha, Nebraska, the same day.

1855 — Libby gave birth to her first child, a son named Frank.

1857 — Libby gave birth to a daughter named Mary Eva, called Mollie.

1859 — Libby and William arrived in Denver City with their two children.

1860 — Denver City and Auraria became one city, Denver.

1859-1860 — Libby helped establish the Ladies Aid Society.

1860 — Libby gave birth to her third child.

— The Byers' house burned to the ground.

1861 — Colorado became a U.S. Territory.

— Charles Nealy Sumner, Libby's eighteen-year old brother, died in Denver.

— Libby's youngest child died.

1862 — Libby and her family moved to a new home near the banks of the Platte River, just south of present-day 6th Avenue.

1864 — Libby gave birth to a baby boy, James Henry Byers.

1864 — The Cherry Creek and Platte River flooded. William's newspaper offices were destroyed.

— The Nathan Hungate family was murdered by Native Americans.

— The Sand Creek Massacre of Arapaho and Cheyenne by troops led by John Chivington.

1865 — Libby's eighteen-month-old son, James, died of pneumonia.

08.01.1876 — Colorado became the 38th state of the United States.

1893 — Libby established the Working Boys Home and School, later renamed the E. M. Byers Home for Boys.

1903 — William Byers died at age 72 in Denver.

1920 — Libby Byers died at age 85 in San Diego, California.

New Words

Annuities: annual payments

Barricade: a temporary wall or similar structure constructed or arranged to prevent people from entering an area

Boomtowns: towns that grow in population quickly

Capsize: overturn a boat in water

Celebrities: famous people

Charitable: assisting those in need

Coma: a state of unconsciousness

Confederacy: the Confederate States of America composed of eleven Southern states that left the United States to fight to preserve slavery. The Confederacy was defeated in the Civil War.

Demented: insane, mentally ill

Depression: an economic downturn that makes it difficult for people to find jobs or earn money

Disillusioned: disappointed

Fordable: a body of water shallow enough to be crossed on foot or on horseback.

Foundation: the structural base of a building

Frontier: an area distant from cities and towns where few people live

Headwaters: the streams at the beginning of a river

Hightailed: moved or traveled fast

Hoax: a made-up story told as fact

Kidnapped: a person taken away illegally or by force

Lobbying: a group of people working together to influence government decisions

Memoir: an account of someone's life written by that person

Morphine: a drug used to relieve pain

Mountain men: trappers and hunters who lived in isolation in the Rocky Mountains prior to the coming of settlers and argonauts

Pathfinders: early explorers

Peace treaty: an agreement between two hostile parties to end a war

Pikes Peak Gold Rush: the rush of people to Colorado in 1859-1860, who came hoping to find gold

Placer gold: nuggets and flakes of gold found in riverbeds

Pneumonia: a serious disease that affects the lungs and makes it difficult to breathe

Prejudices: opinions not based on facts or experiences

Proprietor: a person who owns a business

Prospecting: searching for mineral deposits such as gold or silver

Provisions: food, water, and other supplies needed on a long journey

Quarried: mined, extracted

Quinine: a medicine used to treat malaria

Resin-rich: containing large amounts of tree sap

Retracted: to take something back in writing to correct an inaccurate news item

Scathing: very critical

Seminary: a college or institution where religion and religious matters are taught

Sod houses: a house built of strips of prairie grass roots and dirt

Southern sympathizer: someone who agreed with the Southern states' fight for independence, often someone who wanted slavery to be tolerated by the United States government

Tarnished: metal that has become dull and not shiny

Teamsters: persons who drive teams of horses or other animals to deliver goods

Territory: a part of the United States, not included in any state, with its own elected officials and governing system

Tornadoes: violently rotating columns of air that do significant damage when they touch the ground

Tributary streams: smaller streams that flow into, and become part of, a larger stream or river

Troy ounce: a unit of measurement for weighing precious metals

Union: the states that stayed loyal to the United States government during the American Civil War, also called the North.

Vice: bad or immoral behavior

Vigilante lynching: a person or mob of people who put to death an accused person without a legal trial

Worldly possessions: everything important someone owns

Sources

Bensing, Tom. *Silas Soule: A Short, Eventful Life of Moral Courage.* Indianapolis: Dog Ear Publishing, 2012.

"Byers, William N." In *Encyclopedia of Biography of Colorado.* Chicago: The Century Publishing and Engraving Company, 1901.

Charles River Editors. *The Sand Creek Massacre: The History and Legacy of One of the Indian Wars' Most Notorious Events.* CreateSpace, 2014.

Fossett, Frank. *Colorado: Historical, Descriptive and Statistical Work on the Rocky Mountain Gold and Silver Mining Region.* Denver: Daily Tribune Steam Printing House, 1876.

Hyde, Anne F. "Sam Brannan and Elizabeth Byers: Mormons and Miners at Midcentury." In *Western Lives: A Biographical History of the American West,* edited by Richard W. Etulain. Albuquerque: University of New Mexico Press, 2004.

Lindenbaum, Marilyn. *Discovering Denver: Brick by Brick.* Denver: Historic Denver, Inc., 2012.

Perkin, Robert L. *The First Hundred Years: An Informal History of Denver and the Rocky Mountain News.* Garden City, New York: Doubleday & Company, 1959.

Semple, James Alexander. *Representative Women of Colorado.* Denver: Williamson-Haffner Company, 1914.

Turner, Carol. *Forgotten Heroes & Villains of Sand Creek.* Charleston, South Carolina: The History Press, 2010.

Voynick, Stephen M. *Colorado Gold: From Pike's Peak Rush to the Present.* Missoula, Montana: Mountain Press, 2002.

Zamonski, Stanley W. and Teddy Keller. *The Fifty-Niners: A Denver Diary,* Denver: Sage Books, 1961.

Additional Sources

Beaton, Gail Marjorie, "Making Visible the Invisible: Herstory in Colorado's Queen City," (Thesis, University of Colorado at Denver, 2002).

Byers, Mrs. William N., *The Experiences of One Pioneer Woman.* Unpublished. Denver Public Library, Western History Collection, Box 3, Folder FF 43, Document 427.

"A Pioneer Journalist; or the Founder of the Rocky Mountain News." *Magazine of Western History.* Vol. X, May–October 1889, 50-53.

Report of the John Evans Study Committee, University of Denver: Denver, Colorado, 2014.

Solomon, McKenna C. "The 'Advance Guard of Civilization:' Libby Byers Pioneers Charitable Organizations in Denver," *Colorado Heritage,* November/December 2015, 16-19.

Web Sites

Colorado Chronology, Denver Public Library. https://history. denverlibrary.org/sites/history/files/Colorado%20Chronology%20 11-7-2017.pdf

Encyclopedia Staff, "Colorado Gold Rush," *Colorado Encyclopedia,* last modified January 06, 2018, http://coloradoencyclopedia.org/ article/colorado-gold-rush

Colorado Historic Newspapers Collection, Colorado State Library, https://www.coloradohistoricnewspapers.org/

Colorado State Archives, "Territorial Governors." https://www. colorado.gov/pacific/archives/john-evans

Fairmont Heritage Foundation. "Famous Faces of Fairmount: Libby Byers." http://fairmountheritagefoundation.org/wp-content/uploads/Libby-Byers.pdf

History of Colorado, Volume 4, page 18 for biography of Frank S. Byers, https://books.google.com/books?id=P-hYAAAAMAAJ&pg=PA18&lpg=PA18&dq=marriage+of+Frank+Byers+to+Mart+Sullivan&source=bl&ots=QZZ1m6SRqt&sig=GbqFed40QWD5MJSumY7aW l8uIw0&hl=en&sa=X&ved=2ahUKEwiiw76e6cXcAhWI7IMKHbZ qAO0Q6AEwCHoECAgQAQ#v=onepage&q=marriage%20of%20Frank%20Byers%20to%20Mart%20Sullivan&f=false

Iowa History: An IAGenWeb Special Project, transcribed by Debbie Clough Gerischer, edited by John C. Parish. http://iagenweb.org/history/palimpsest/1920-Dec.htm

History Net Magazines. Sand Creek Massacre articles. http://www.historynet.com/sand-creek-massacre

William Byers: Founder of the Rocky Mountain News, Colorado Virtual Library, https://www.coloradovirtuallibrary.org/digital-colorado/colorado-histories/beginnings/william-byers-founder-of-the-rocky-mountain-news/

1860 Census Data, Mortality Statistics. https://www2.census.gov/library/publications/decennial/1860/statistics/1860d-03.pdf

Index

Married Woman's Property Act, 70
Merrick, John, 19, 20, 21
Muscatine, Iowa, 1, 3, 65

Oakes, D. C., 22
Omaha, Nebraska, 4, 5, 6, 7, 16, 17,
    24, 28
Oregon Trail, 24-25, 26, 33, 66

Pikes Peak Gold Rush, 9
Platte River, 9, 18, 26, 27, 49, 50,
    51, 52, 66
Pony Express, 47

Rocky Mountain News, 17-19, 21,
    23-24, 30, 41-42, 50, 51,
    52, 55, 74, 75
Russell, William Greene, 9

Sand Creek Massacre, 54-55, 61, 62
Sumner, Charles, 17, 47-48

Wootton, "Uncle Dick", 19, 34

Acknowledgments

A book is written by a single author, but as with all authors, I had lots of help. This biography wouldn't have been possible without the help of librarians at the Denver Public Library, Western History Collection. They helped me research Elizabeth Byers and taught me how to use the DPL-WHC archives. It was in the archives I found Elizabeth Byers' memoir, *The Experiences of One Pioneer Woman,* which made me decide to write this book.

To learn about Elizabeth Byers' early life in Ohio and Iowa, I was assisted by Shelia Choudoin, a local historian from the Musser Public Library, and Bob Casari from the Ross County Genealogical Society. Jan Gunia, a friend and local historian, helped me research Elizabeth Byers through different websites. She also came with me to the Fairmount Cemetery and helped me find Libby's grave.

Finally, I'd like to thank my critique group, 30th Street Fiction, and the beta readers who helped me edit and improve the manuscript. I'd especially like to thank Carol Silloway, former fifth grade teacher; Sarah-Finch Rollins, beta reader extraordinaire; Michael Erikson, Byers-Evans House Museum; Mary George; and, of course, my mother, Joyce Bell, who has always read anything and everything I've ever written.

About the Author

Author J.v.L. Bell is a Colorado native who grew up climbing fourteeners, exploring old ghost towns, and enjoying stories from Colorado's vibrant past. Her first novel, *The Lucky Hat Mine,* was published in October 2016, and intertwines historical events and historical characters into a fun historical mystery set in 1863, Idaho Springs. *Elizabeth Byers: Denver Pioneer* is her first non-fiction book.

Contact J.v.L. Bell through her website www. jvlbell.com or by emailing her at Julie@JvLBell.com. Julie enjoys sharing her historical research at schools and libraries and is always happy to hear from her readers.